WONDERFUL NATURAL WONDERS

THE GRAND CANYON

BY BRAY JACOBSON

Gareth Stevens PUBLISHING

Please visit our website, www.garethstevens.com. For a free color catalog of all our high-quality books, call toll free 1-800-542-2595 or fax 1-877-542-2596.

Library of Congress Cataloging-in-Publication Data
Names: Jacobson, Bray, author.
Title: The grand canyon / Bray Jacobson.
Description: New York : Gareth Stevens Publishing, [2023] | Series: Wonderful natural wonders | Includes index.
Identifiers: LCCN 2021036625 (print) | LCCN 2021036626 (ebook) | ISBN 9781538276785 (set) | ISBN 9781538276792 (library binding) | ISBN 9781538276778 (paperback) | ISBN 9781538276808 (ebook)
Subjects: LCSH: Grand Canyon (Ariz.)–Juvenile literature.
Classification: LCC F788 .J165 2023 (print) | LCC F788 (ebook) | DDC 979.1/32–dc23
LC record available at https://lccn.loc.gov/2021036625
LC ebook record available at https://lccn.loc.gov/2021036626

Published in 2023 by
Gareth Stevens Publishing
29 E. 21st Street
New York, NY 10010

Designer: Tanya Dellaccio
Editor: Kristen Nelson

Photo credits: Cover Keneva Photography/Shutterstock.com; background texture (pp 3-24) BEMPhoto_31/Shutterstock.com; p. 5 Martin M303 /Shutterstock.com; p. 7 (background) arigato/Shutterstock.com; p. 7 (map) BigMouse/Shutterstock.com; p. 9 Sean Pavone/Shutterstock.com; p. 11 kojihirano/Shutterstock.com; p. 13 Paul B. Moore/Shutterstock.com; p. 15 Dominic Gentilcore PhD/Shutterstock.com; p. 17 Lynn Yeh/Shutterstock.com; p. 19 Studio Barcelona/Shutterstock.com; p. 21 Galyna Andrushko/Shutterstock.com.

Printed in the United States of America

CPSIA compliance information: Batch #CSGS23: For further information contact Gareth Stevens, New York, New York at 1-800-542-2595.

CONTENTS

The Largest Canyon 4
How It Formed 8
Wide and Deep 10
Layers of Rock 12
The National Park 16
Fun in the Canyon 20
Glossary 22
For More Information 23
Index 24

Boldface words appear in the glossary.

The Largest Canyon

Canyons are landforms that form because of rivers, **erosion**, and the movement of Earth's **tectonic plates**. They have **steep** sides and deep, commonly narrow, valleys. The Grand Canyon is the largest canyon in the United States! It's a natural wonder.

The Grand Canyon is in the northern part of Arizona. It runs from the Paria River to Grand Wash Cliffs, which is almost to the state of Nevada. It's 277 miles (446 km) long. The Colorado River runs through it.

IDAHO
WYOMING
NEVADA
UTAH
COLORADO
CALIFORNIA
GRAND CANYON
NEW MEXICO
ARIZONA
COLORADO RIVER

How It Formed

The Colorado **Plateau** formed as Earth's tectonic plates were lifted many millions of years ago. The Colorado River flows through the plateau. Over time, it wore away the rock. This created the Grand Canyon. It may be 5 million to 70 million years old!

Wide and Deep

At its widest, the Grand Canyon is 18 miles (29 km) wide! It's narrowest width is 525 feet (160 m). The deepest spot in the Grand Canyon is 1 mile (1.6 km) deep. That's more than 17 football fields deep!

Layers of Rock

The wearing away of rock in the Grand Canyon **revealed** rock layers. While the canyon looks mostly red, these layers are gray, pink, and even green. Scientists use these rock layers to learn about the past.

Scientists use the rock to tell how the **climate** of the canyon has changed over time. They discovered past plants and animals that lived there through **fossils**. The rock layers of the Grand Canyon are part of why it's called a natural wonder!

The National Park

The Grand Canyon has long been **recognized** as a natural wonder. Parts of the canyon were first **protected** by the U.S. government in 1893. It became a national park in 1919. Even more land around it was added to the park in 1975.

GRAND CANYON
NATIONAL PARK
NATIONAL
PARK
SERVICE

Grand Canyon National Park is full of plants and animals! There are more than 350 kinds of birds, including bald eagles. Foxes, rabbits, and badgers also live there. Cacti and many kinds of trees are found throughout the park.

CACTI

Fun in the Canyon

The Grand Canyon is a natural wonder known throughout the world. More than 6 million people visit Grand Canyon National Park every year! They go hiking, fishing, and camping. Some take boat trips down the Colorado River!

GLOSSARY

climate: the average weather conditions of a place over a period of time

erosion: the act of wearing away by water, wind, or ice

fossil: the marks or remains of plants and animals that formed over thousands or millions of years

plateau: a large area of land with raised sides and a level top

protect: to keep safe

recognize: to know and remember

reveal: to make able to be seen

steep: almost straight up and down

tectonic plate: one of the moveable masses of rock that create Earth's surface

FOR MORE INFORMATION

BOOKS

Koestler-Grack, Rachel. *Arizona.* Minneapolis, MN: Bellwether Media, Inc., 2022.

London, Martha. *Looking into the Grand Canyon.* Mankato, MN: The Child's World, 2020.

WEBSITES

Be A Junior Ranger
www.nps.gov/grca/learn/kidsyouth/beajuniorranger.htm
Do you want to help protect natural wonders like the Grand Canyon? Become a junior ranger with the National Park Service!

Grand Canyon National Park
kids.nationalgeographic.com/nature/article/grand-canyon
Find out more about visiting the Grand Canyon here.

INDEX

age 8

Arizona 6

Colorado Plateau 6

Colorado River 6, 8

fossils 14

national park 16, 18

Nevada 6

size 10

tectonic plates 4, 8

United States 4

visitors 20

wildlife 18